HAIKU FROM THE HEART

by

Sylvia Jones

is book is dedicated to my mom, Ellen Saelg, who reignited my spark to write again. It was in
r time of illness and dying that writing helped me cope with all that I encountered and helped
me remain grounded. Also, to family members, especially my son, Cliff, who has been
luential in urging me to get these Haiku into a book. To my "Tribe Writer" on line friends lead
by Jeff Goins, to Day Kelly for all his love and inspiration, and especially to my friend,
colleague and fellow writer, Michelle McCrackin. Our paths in life keep crossing. I am so
rtunate and blessed to have a soul sister who is so passionate about writing. Thank you for all
our encouragement and in helping with the process of getting my collection into my very first
book. Your friendship and professionalism mean a lot to me.

Chapter 1: Haiku about Haiku & Mom's Inspiration

Chapter 2: Sand, Sun, Surf, Nature

Chapter 3 : The Dark Place

Chapter 4: Hodgepodge of Everything In-Between

Chapter 1:
Five, seven, five count
emotions onto paper
haiku poetry

Napping in the chair
resting her eyes and her soul
every breath struggles

Her mind now wanders
she was once very brilliant
where? what? when? she asks

Once two hundred pounds
now every bone can be felt
wasting away slow

Every weekend out
shopping, eating, having fun
visit Tallwoods now

Youth caring for old
rushing through, not listening
she cries for patience

In the past few years
my emotions up and down
her health good then poor

Many shoe styles
Emelda's twin with the shoes
now feet bandaged up

She enjoyed the sun
tanning, skin creams, fighting age
time won with wrinkles

The roles are now changed
feeding, toileting, cleaning
she feels like a child

She still holds on now
not ready to give it up
grasping on to hope

Cannot concentrate
every thought, moment is her
will my calm return?

Exhaustion creeps in
taking all my energy
making me depressed

Surreptitiously
death will consume her body

no more suffering

All I want to do
is cry, cry and cry some more
watching her suffer.

Oh how beautiful
to really know her inside
enduring hardships

Feeling so helpless
she had done so much for me
cannot turn back time

All the years of moves
A traveling vagabond
nearing the end point

When Harry left us
she lost a piece of her heart
never to be found

Heartfelt misery
day in and out just waiting
time drags on and on

The inner sanctum
the place to be safe and calm
let peace prevail here

The smell of her death
lingers lightly in my nose
it will be soon now

Final resting place

all of her fears are gone now
the first day of spring

Hard to close my eyes
visions of her suffering
still fresh in my mind

I was there for her
memories linger about
it was hard to watch

She saw me crying
true human spirit prevailed
helping her through this

It has hit her hard
the eldest daughter, my sis
many sleepless nights

My brother so strong
his emotions tucked inside
the surface is thin

Will he allow it
the true feelings to come out
natural response

How long will it take
emotions to calm, relax
resolve to settle

Sadness takes over
making me lazy to walk
how awful is that?

The yelling echoes
the sadness rushes back in
trying to let go

The cold dining room
I still feel it on my skin
see it in my mind

Get on with my life
that is what everyone says
she was a big piece

It has been a week
feels like an eternity
we miss her so much

Total exhaustion
overtook her whole body
drifting off to sleep.

Over and over
my mind is in replay mode
time will not erase

Other thoughts in view
I was thankful to be there
yet impact remains

Scent of hyacinths
feeling Goosebumps head to toe
her presence was felt

Strange experience
as if she were in the car
I cried tears of joy

To feel her right there
longing for a hug and kiss
love and miss you Mom

A field of flowers
floating above looking down
it was just a dream

The day was so odd
not having her here with us
celebrate Mothers!

Quiet solitude
at the memorial park
resting in peace now

The scent of mother
so strong in the car last night
she stopped to visit

I just cried at first
found myself talking to her
spirits never die

The pain will ease up
now that I know she visits
watches over me

Eyelids so heavy
I will try to get some rest
wiping the slate clean

Slumber is coming
a much needed refreshment

under the covers

Starting a new day
each one better than the last
dawn bringing sunshine

Told him I would sleep
feeling his arms around me
so I toss and turn

Hard for all of us
in one way or another
coping as we can

A headache coming
fighting off needed sleep time
my eyes are closing

I will regret it
not succumbing to sleep time
bleary-eyed morning

Must go to sleep now
forcing myself into bed
please be quiet head

Some much needed sleep
just seems to escape me now
sadness flooding through

Time will relieve it
feelings of chaos inside
seems not soon enough

My life will go on

but without her around now
my heart feels a void

Ashes in the niche
your spirit survives, protects
always by our side

Beautiful Sunday
at the memorial park
peace and solitude

Outside the chapel
someone kneeling and talking
missing their loved one

You would visit him
remembering good and bad
times spent with Harry

So, so quiet here
the distant parkway traffic
barely audible

Bench under the tree
sitting on it, reflecting
absorbed by nature

Breeze gently blowing
birds singing, crickets chipping
they are the life here

Is he really there?
the shadow only she sees
waiting to take her

No need for the pills
searching the mind, let it flow
ink onto paper

It cuts like a knife
all reality must end
truth is razor sharp

Sleep eternally
no thoughts, no pain, no anguish
peaceful and serene

Ready to let go
remember the good and bad
treasured memories

Feeling the turmoil
headaches, stomach knots, pressure
wishing sleep would help

Tossing and turning
visions, noise and dreams invade
when will the night end?

I am her angel
she wrote this down on paper
baby me, brown eyes

Chapter 2:

The winds have picked up
sand flies lightly through the air
sticky granules

Fog enshrouded moon
restricting rays of lightness
dark Ocean below

Crickets are chirping
dogs barking, surf is flowing
not in harmony

Doorstep dragonfly
struggles to hold onto life
but it is too late

Evening on the porch
taking in the sights and sounds
as night passes by

Cold-blooded gecko
stretching out on the lattice
warming up a bit

Dolphins are diving
lunching on a school of fish
frolic in the sea

The clouds passing by
figures of people and things
imagination

Sitting in the rain
watching him boogie boarding
the waves are awesome

View from the front porch
the blue ocean straight ahead

dunes, sand, waves, blue sky

Renters row, lined up
street by street, nautical names
all on vacation

Sand between my toes
cold and soft, almost mud like
leaving footprints path

Crab out of his hole
madly waving sharp white claws
gets swept into waves

Pink, blue, light purple
colors in the evening sky
nightfall settles in

Moonlight through the clouds
glimmers on the black ocean
the new dawn to come

Flickering pier lights
signals an end to the day
evening colors form

On the waters edge
seagulls and feathered friends skim
along the tides foam

Gulls glide by with ease
kites dance around in the breeze
wind catches just so

Water so dark blue

surf breaking gently on shore
soothing feelings ebb

Boat in the distance
fish entrapped in the netting
fresh for dinner's plate

Alone on the beach
gentle breeze blows through the dune
this is solitude

Peaceful reflections
of days gone by, the present
and dreams to come true

Sea gulls flying by
pelicans diving for food
spreading wings to sail

No end in the view
looking into the ocean
stretching far beyond

Inner balance, peace
lost in the thick clouded woods
need to find the light

One with the water
never expecting the rain
let sunshine follow

Florida sunshine
tanning bodies by the pool
palm tree breezes below

The light of day dims
the horizon opens up
swallows evening sun

Tapestry of sky
colors pink, blue, light yellow
sunset time is near

Glad winter is gone
absorbing the rays of warmth
first day at the beach

Relax with each breath
tethered emotions unwind
flowing through the waves

Blueness of the sky
becomes enveloped by white
clouds stretching out long

The colors of spring
all about new beginnings
green growth, a fresh start

The crisp morning air
inhaling freshness of life
taking on the day.

Solace at the beach
worries swept away in waves
Mmany shades of clouds

The sun is teasing
hiding behind outstretched clouds
peeking out by chance

Gentle breeze blowing
no humidity at all
the perfect setting

Sand, sun, water, dunes
the office space without walls
inspires to write

No peace and quiet
radio on, kids yelling
ocean drowns all sounds

Inside a cocoon
enveloped in calm feelings
warmth filtering in

Last day to sun bathe
before the long ride back home
pouring rain, no sun

Storm clouds are lifting
no further attempts to tan
ready to go home

Smell the sea sprayed air
wave sounds relax the body
warming the spirit

Never ending flow
blue, white, rolling in and out
these are ocean waves

Breeze blows through] the air
moist sand in between your toes

evening at the beach

Lone pelican glides
gentle breeze sways through the marsh
glimmering sunshine

Many shades of blue
puffy clouds float by slowly
sky is a canvas

Sea gulls crying out
hovering along the pier
disrupt the calm surf

Graceful blue heron
hidden within the marsh land
so quiet, stands tall

Winter on the beach
wind ruffles seagull's feathers
sand sprays through the dunes

The humidity
a thick blanket of hot heat
suffocates your breath

Goat Island round up
from fall until springs return
marsh walk tradition

Cold and wet morning
rain has fallen all night long
dampening the mood

Wind whipping through trees

the ocean thrashing about
Mother Nature's wrath

Full moon through skylight
is dim gray patch of color
on the bathroom floor

Chapter 3: The Dark Place

Deep dark hopelessness
the cavern of depression
do not let me fall!

The tower of strength
weak unsteady pressure builds
loosening the bond

The still of the night
my thoughts overpowering
yields to shedding tears

Dangling on a string
his movements orchestrated
the puppet dances

Such mixed emotions
strewn like a jig saw puzzle
picking up pieces

My life as it seems
stuck in a holding pattern
finding the new me

Frustration building
emotions stirred up inside
heart breaks either way

Express your feelings
the silence is deafening
it infuriates

Appearing happy
smothered in the shroud of lies
fake relationship

Solitude of thoughts
memories crash through the mind
trickle of teardrops

Strong family rock
sent plunging over the edge
is now a dirt pile

Secretly had wished
that he would have changed his mind
divorce is final

You cannot see that
being there as a father
means more than money

Walking on eggshells
always feeling second best
breaking of the heart

Time passes quickly
cherish the moments with care
blink and it is gone

Lately wondering
what happened to my daughter
time changes people

Life is not perfect
challenges, choices, changes
do the best you can

Sadness in the soul
harbors darkness in the heart
depression prevails

Tears welled up inside
the flow is never ending
drowning in the flood

Hard to figure out
hieroglyphics of feelings
one day at a time

Saddening the heart
love should be priority
nothing else matters

The fiber of self
dissipates and fades away
memories are gone

Wrapped in loneliness
missing you, heart hurts inside
tender touch sheds all

Daddy's little girl
still wrapped around his finger

Mom does not matter

Patience wearing thin
emotions drain from body
time for a new path

Feelings tossed aside
being taken for granted
a mere after thought

Since final divorce
spirit and soul feel a void
total emptiness

It is personal
thirty-six years together
our bond now broken

First it was fleeting
loneliness makes me feel dead
soul a lifeless corpse

So uninspired
just cannot find the right words
lacking expression

Slipping in slowly
darkness is a jagged knife
pierces loneliness

Resentment, grudges
eat away at every nerve
body, mind, spirit

Tossing and turning

missing arms holding me tight
love is not secure

It had to be me
something he really despised
to just let go of

No peace within self
the healing will be complete
need to forgive him

Manipulation
seemly unaware of
head lost in the clouds

Tears flow, heart still breaks
hurtful feelings penetrate
no shield of armor

Two become as one
thought it would be forever
wedding vows shattered

My heart falls apart
said you would always be here
promise is broken

Weighing on my heart
lack of sensitivity
self centered vision

Feeling a deep void
in the abyss of my soul
echoes emptiness

In stillness of time
yearning for the love I knew
missing our moments

Marriage is balance
bond between husband and wife
the priority

Never really thought
heart could actually break
soul mates no longer

Forced realization
have to know it is not me
gave my total soul

The sadness creeps in
try to fight it and be strong
tears build up inside

Happy memories
the only source of comfort
heart still feels the sting

Relationship ends
heart full of cracks, crevices
where love used to be

To reconsider
window of time has run out
the door is now closed

No substitution
for parent time never spent
with your own children

Chapter 4: Hodgepodge of everything in between

We cannot escape
each day as it comes and goes
make the best of it

Aging does happen
body wearing down, mind fades
but stay young at heart

Sound of the box fan
reverberates otherwise
what would be silence

With all of his heart
The Crooked Spoon Gastro Pub
this was Steven's dream

Theater of Life
memories of roles gone by
brighten the spirit

Our love has grown strong
standing here at the altar
we say our "I Do's"

Loving each other
our two hearts becoming one
now husband and wife

Music resonates
soul is touched by every note

let your spirit soar

On our wedding day
every fiber of my soul
I will give to you

Not a perfect art
challenges, hugs and kisses
this is motherhood

December is here
year is coming to an end
hope for love and peace

Jingle bells ringing
Christmas carolers singing
the season is here

Focus to ponder
no resolutions just goals
make it as great year

My special grandson
always smiling and laughing
you warm up my heart

Write with brevity
rough draft, remove extra words
keep it to the point

Music serenades
fingers flowing over keys
calming violin

Interpretation

jubilation or sadness
depends on the piece

Playing Violin
sharing virtuosity
prodigal beauty

Surrender to God
he has a plan and the path
just have to believe

Chasing the brass ring
life passes by, health suffers
a tough price to pay

Creativity
everybody has something
we are all unique

Here for a reason
compassion, patience and strength
deep down in the soul

The mind's light bulb dims
flickering of frustrations
having no control

Seeking life's balance
movement, living, relaxing
being true to self

Senior citizens
deserving of attention
brighten aging souls

For success and growth
reach the spirit deep within
see your efforts shine

Smoke those cigarettes
no thoughts about your future
gasping to the grave

Follow her advice
take care of your health always
NO SMOKING ALLOWED

You think you are cool
taking a drag, blowing smoke
snuffing out your life

We all get older
smoking catches up to you
who is your angel?

Two leaders or more
you cannot get enough air
struggle, breath no more

Help! I cannot breath
you do not know what it is
she said while dying

Being a mother
many years before you grasp
the intensity

(8-23-13- published in On More Monmouth Musings Blog- Re: Topless Day)

Baring upper chest
standing up for equal rights
woman verses man

This one is an ode to an on-line writing group:

Strong community
penning thoughts, supportive friends
we are Tribe Writers

An Estonian haiku. The pattern is 4-6-4

Head uut aastat   Happy New Year
Parima tervise   Best of Health
Unistused   Dreams come true

Additional Authors haiku:

Cliff Jones   Today is your day
(My Son)   May everything be special
                           Happy Birthday Mom!

elgi Vannell Willis   South Carolina
My Sister)   the dream of warmer weather
                                 waiting for sunshine

Loss of a loved one
my Sis, the life preserver
relieved of sad thoughts

Where did the sun go
so sick of the falling snow
makes your spirit low

It's April Fools Day
the pranksters are out to play
watch your back, I say

Brain feeling like lead
stop the rhyming in my head
time to go to bed

<u>The History of Haiku</u>

Haiku is a poetic form an a type of poetry from Japanese culture that originated around the 17th century.

Haiku themes include nature, feelings or experiences. It is amazing how much emotion can be packed into three lines!

<u>You too can haiku: follow the syllable sequence.</u>

5____

7____

5____

*

5____

7____

5____

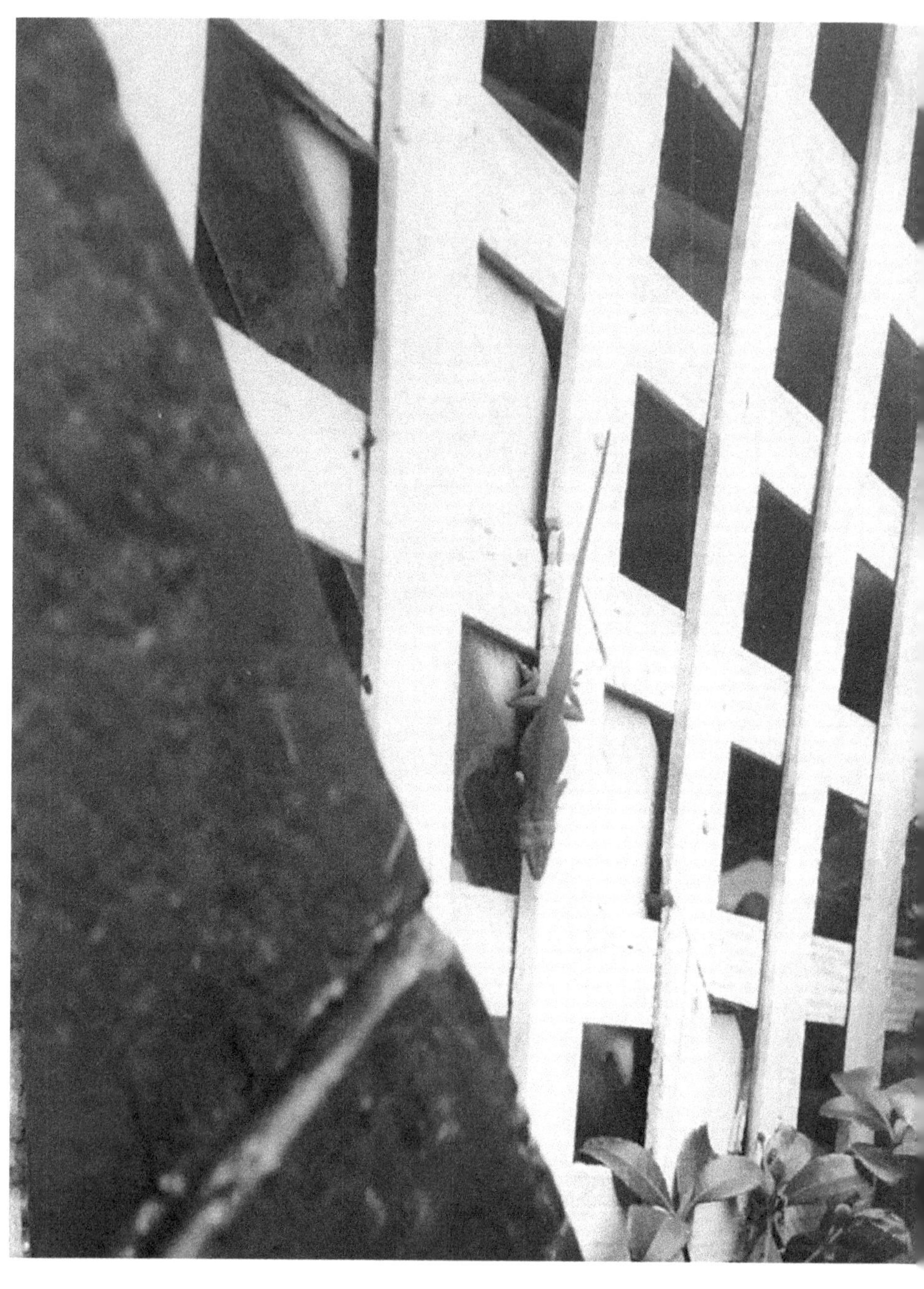

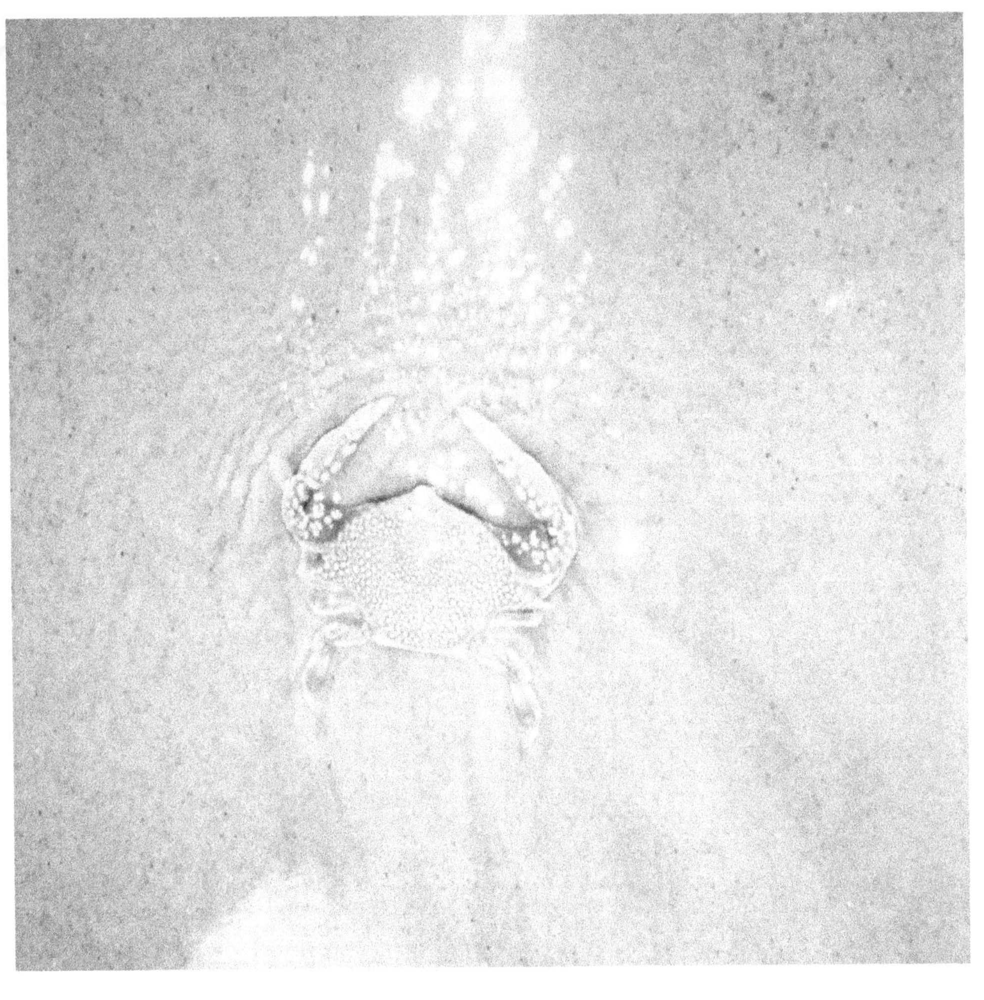

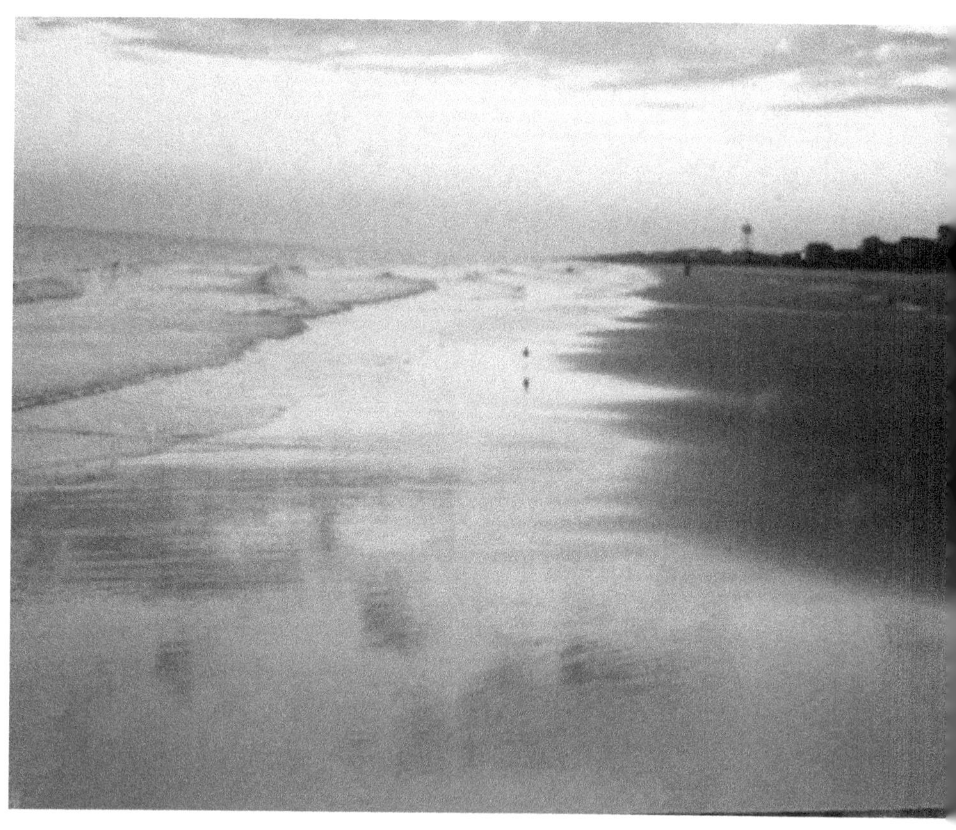

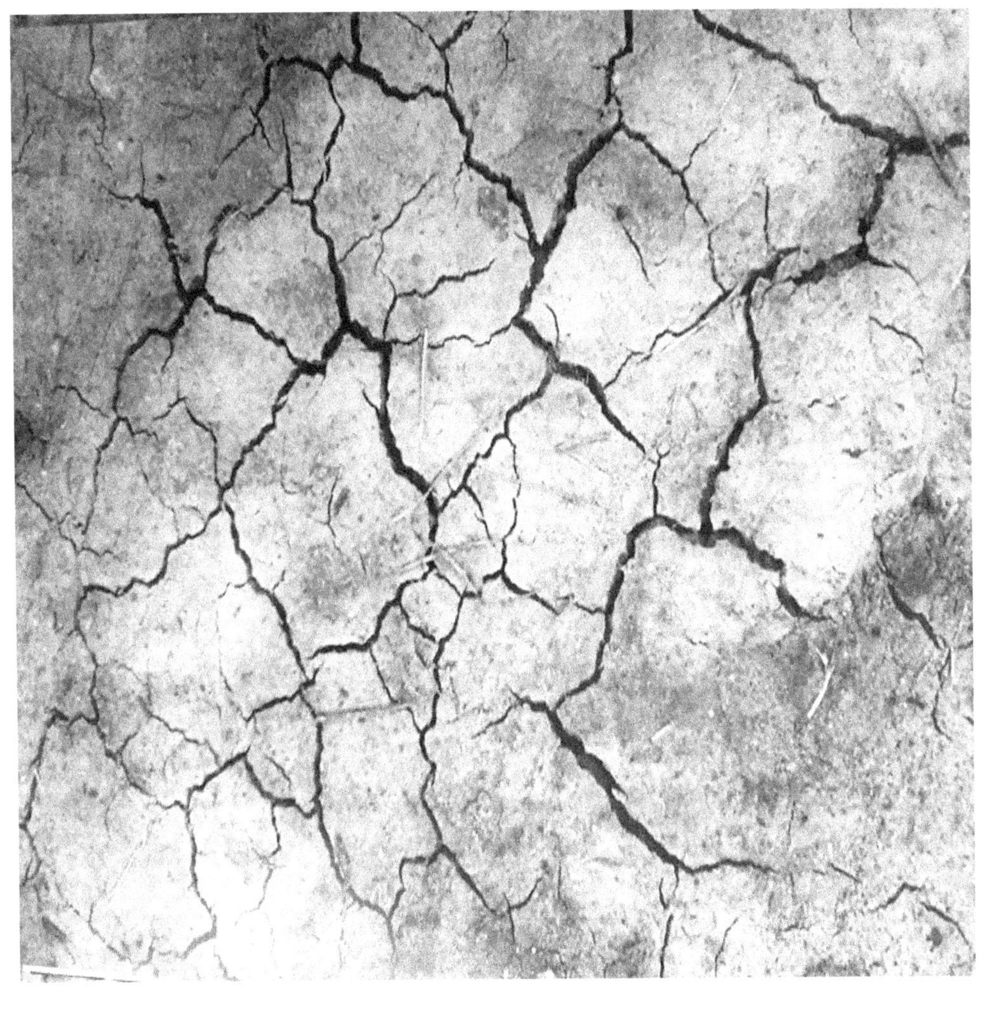

Gecko (Holden Beach N.C.)

Crab (Holden Beach N.C.)

Beach scene (Holden Beach N.C.)

Cracks in the mud (Myrtle Beach S.C.)

Smiling Jack (visiting Indiana)

Love in the sand (Huntington Beach S.C.)

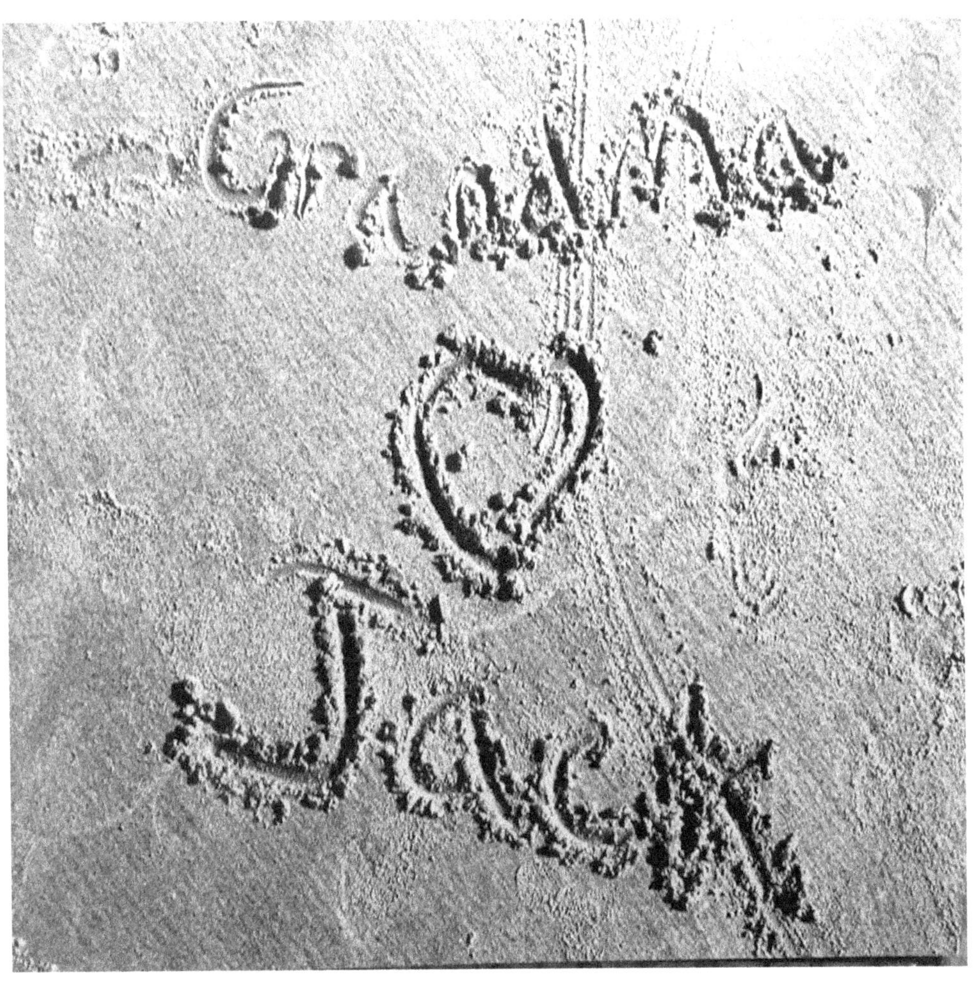

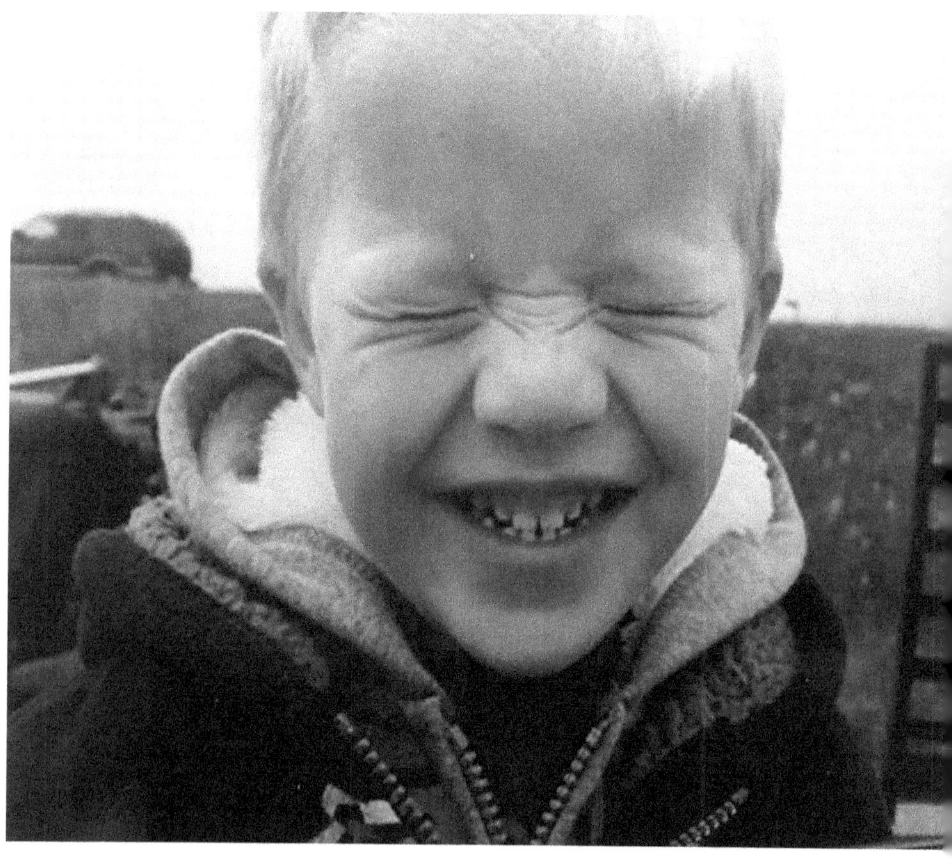

www.ingramcontent.com/pod-product-compliance
Lightning Source LLC
Chambersburg PA
CBHW050627070726
47592CB00028B/1826